MAN
ANIMAL
THING

ALFRED
SCHAFFER

MAN
ANIMAL
THING

TRANSLATED BY **MICHELE HUTCHISON**

 **EYEWEAR** PUBLISHING

First published in 2021
by Eyewear Publishing Ltd / Black Spring Press Group
Suite 333, 19-21 Crawford Street
Marylebone, London W1H 1PJ
United Kingdom

Typeset with graphic design by Edwin Smet
Author photograph Luke Kuisis
Printed in England by TJ Books Ltd, Padstow, Cornwall

*The publisher gratefully acknowledges the support of
the Dutch Foundation for Literature*

Nederlands
letterenfonds
dutch foundation
for literature

MIX
Paper from
responsible sources
FSC   FSC® C013056
www.fsc.org

WWW.EYEWEARPUBLISHING.COM

TRANSLATOR'S NOTE

In *Man Animal Thing* poet Alfred Schaffer presents a blurred revisionist biography of South African king Shaka Zulu whose tumultuous life spanned four decades from 1787 to 1828. Far from being a straight historical telling, Schaffer employs a form of channeling, juxtaposing Shaka's experiences with his own. It is hard for the reader to tell where the poet stops and the warrior begins. Deliberately creating anachronistic settings for his character such as a quiz show and an airport, and giving Shaka different guises such as that of a dog, Schaffer adds humour and a contemporary sensibility to the work which is experimental while remaining very readable and narrative-driven. The tone is an easy rhythmical parlando with a few conscious changes of register, both toward the more formal and toward the more vernacular.

•

Alfred Schaffer is of Aruban-Dutch origin and was born in the Netherlands in 1973. He lives in South Africa where he teaches at Stellenbosch University. He has won many prizes for his six poetry collections, most recently the prestigious P.C. Hooft oeuvre prize, and also garnered acclaim for his translations of Antje Krog's poems.

'Je continue comme j'ai commence, pour la beauté du geste.'
'La beauté, on dit qu'elle est dans l'oeil, dans l'oeil de celui qui regarde.'
Alors si personne ne regarde plus?

Holy Motors (2012)

A BLACK MAN ARMED WITH A SPEAR CAUSED A
COMMOTION DURING YESTERDAY'S EVENING RUSH
HOUR. HE PROSTRATED HIMSELF ACROSS THE
MOTORWAY. THE MOTORWAY RAN RIGHT
THROUGH THE MAN'S PLACE OF ABODE.

Drivers struggled to avoid the man.
The man was under the influence, according to the police.
But what does that mean, 'under the influence'.
A good question, actually, it's such a broad concept.
Under the influence, he appeared aggressive and confused.
It took some real effort to finally apprehend the man.
The police had to resort to physical violence to handcuff him.
It's hard to imagine that he is still alive so let us pray.

HARD FACTS ABOUT SHAKA, IN OTHER WORDS HARD FACTS ABOUT ME

Because the facts, they have to be laid on the table.
Name: Shaka. S-H-A-K-A. Exactly as you say it.
First fact. I'm based on all kinds of things
but not on the truth — *yeah kiddo, you'd love that, wouldn't you?*
my mother used to say.

What a coincidence that I was born in Africa!
Africa is big and dry, sometimes it rains in Africa
is Africa a country, I don't think so.
Who knows, Africa may be the orphan of the world economy.
The first man learned to hop and skip here but
what does the 8,512,784,325,236,108,946,347[th] person know about Africa?

I'm a blank screen, a black warrior
with ebony skin and a transparent soul.
On my Facebook profile pic I'm Napoleon
my left foot rests on a servant's head.

I have raised and saved a nation.
My father was called He Who Has Good Reasons For What He Does.
A man never takes the floor in his father's presence
except when his father asks him something.
I'm not much of a family man, my birth
was a scandal, dry humping that got out of hand.

'Look, a UFO.' My first words.
According to rumours, I was conceived during Mardi Gras.
Other rumours say that I was begotten in a river.
The best version, I think, is the one about the night-time car park
right in the heart of the tundra.

I use Makassaroil™ to cover the grey hairs.
Good stuff, not sticky and it doesn't stain.
According to sources, I'm six foot four, according to others
I've got a hunchback and a speech defect.
Usain Bolt, Jess Owens: mediocre runners.
According to eye witnesses I bludgeoned a leopard
to pulp as a young teen.
According to others, I was teased about my tiny cock.

An entire herd of water buffalo was used
to film the slaughter of a single buffalo in *Apocalypse Now*.
I know more than a hundred names for 'water buffalo'.
I only know one for 'woman'.

The short-handed stabbing spear, that's my invention.
'The *assegaai*'s blade was longer than that of a regular spear – 45
centimetres long and almost 4 centimetres wide – it was attached to
a strong, short shaft. Shaka called this spear *iklwa*, after the sucking
noise it made when it was pulled out of a body after having been
thrust in it deeply.' End of quote.

How many facts so far? Just a few more then
everything that exists around us is hand-made.
Mountains, snakes and rivers, everything inanimate and animate.
Everything outside of my territory is one big wasteland:
if [x] has to be killed then [x] will be killed
because [x] has nowhere to go.
When I see the vultures circling high above my head
I think Look at that, the king's birds are hungry!
And so I feed them.

I came on a boat from Africa to tell my story
a small boat carrying lots of people.
The odd person fell overboard along the way

it gave some relief but never for long.
Although we sailed on the open seas, it stank of cheese
and shit and alcohol on our boat
I also lost my favourite spear there.

I'm the legitimate heir of The Tramp, aka
He Who Has Problems.
My favourite kit: a t-shirt and jeans
during the week, a turban and animal skin
on formal occasions.

Betray me and you betray my people.
Leading a nation of people is like pruning a garden.
The more you prune
the stronger the tree, the fuller the shrub.

An army is a starving monster, you have to keep feeding it.
My people had no idea.
On the battlefield there was some shouting back and forth
and a bit of rolling around, an idiotic chaos.
OK, *cut!* I shouted, this is just silly.
From that day onwards blood began to flow.

When everything was pretty much conquered, on the even days
death and I played eenie meenie miney mo.
I categorically refused door-to-door advertising.
When I wanted water I shouted Sister, water please!
I stopped reading the papers but I still watched sport and MTV
and I still kept a diary.

Fact: Martin Scorsese filmed almost every scene in *Raging Bull*
in black and white because of all the blood.
Yet there's only ten minutes of actual boxing in the whole film.

I hear you ask But how does it work in practice.
With all those henchmen all that overtime?
Well, they work fast
a) break neck b) bash in skull c) impale the shit.
A head deeply impaled on a spike, now there
you have something resembling orgasm's famous face.

A leader without followers is a ghost
a ghost is like a restless spirit.
And what it's like death death death is pure television
complete bullshit, the script is crap
don't believe death death death.

'People who were found guilty of sorcery were impaled through
 the anus using a series of short, pointed stakes until the neck
was reached; after that they were abandoned to die in the veldt,
prey to vultures and hyenas.' End of quote.

For a promotional film I stood in a vat filled with ice
for almost three hours, all kinds of stuff went wrong, the lights went out
the catering went on strike, the director drowned.
I had just one line but what a line it was.
While in operettas all of the text has to be sung!

Each day I feel like I've drunk five bottles of wine
I float like vermicelli in a big pan of soup.
The soup is lukewarm with a layer of fat on top.

When I have guests, I pretend to be deaf.
'Just you see – when he's had his coffee
he'll start banging on about the war again.'

I still haven't settled on my final words.
What's going on, children of my fatherland? (Too weak.)
Are you killing me, king of the earth? (Too friendly.)
Let me be your servant! (Has already been said once.)

When I die this country will be occupied from all sides
by the shrewd white man, then we'll see something
mark my words! (Not sure I can remember all of that.)

What do I see when I look in the mirror? An undulating reflection
of a reflection of a reflection.
I call this the Droste effect
you call it Symbolism.

Last fact.
I am not dead.
Try to prove it.

YOU'VE GOT SOURCES AND SOURCES – SO
WHERE TO START.
Maybe simply in nature, first there was nothing
but water, woods, sand and grass, a mountain range
as long as the Great Wall of China.
A country squeezed between two seas.
It was neither hot nor cold
the wastelands were lacking in figures of speech.
Here the first man was found, black and steaming
and baffled he suddenly lay there, full on meteorite.
Anyone born into this world found their grave ready dug.
The soil was rich, sometimes a person would find
an animal lying dead in a field and would speak to it.
That same person would strike
when looking for food, with friendly hostility.
Anyone who killed a snake would be sent into the future.
There where it was marshy and pitch black, you just walked
until you were exhausted and happy if you found a dry place
where you could lay down for a while.

But mainly it was a pretty empty place.
'Empty' is a complicated concept.
After all, 'empty' isn't the opposite of 'full'.

For a long time, things went uphill, we'll
skip some episodes and behold, in full regalia
the father of the hero of this tale.
Half an eye on the sultry lady pushing perfume
on the advertising hoardings along the road and one eye
on his brand new girlfriend, future mother
and a real catch by the looks of it, her bare feet

up on the dashboard and her sexy curves effortlessly stuffed
into a gold-coloured bikini from the brand Memento.
She trims her fingernails, he drives too fast
this is foolish bravado, youthfulness most likely
the new era, as the saying goes
this is his fourth bride but lips sealed
she is forbidden by law, the radio is on full.
She can sing well and is an excellent dancer, intoxicates him
in the darkness but above all they are related – trouble will come of that.
A son for example, heralded by an ancestor
disguised as a snake who one fine day
slips into their hut, a snake in a house
is best left alone, you ask what he wants to eat, drink
you talk to him and act interested.

The son's fingers are almost cold
soon his whole hand will follow and then the rest.
But we're getting ahead of the ending.
First the break of day and night and day
and night and again and again until you can see Death.
There he sits, sipping an espresso.
Waiting at your kitchen table.

I draw a picture with my coloured pencils.
A square house a couple of hours' drive from the coast.
A lovely roof on top, there's still some people to be added.
People who don't look sad, nor happy, one of them at least.
Outside a car is hitting its brakes.
Also a deep ditch in which you can drown.
With mudfish and a doll floating in circles.
And flowers towering along the banks.
Gaping like rubberneckers.
I hear a car door slam, shouting, bellowing –
that's the wind, it's just the wind
this is already my tenth attempt
the house has neither windows nor a door, though
it can't be all that difficult.
It was a scorching day, I remember that much.
The roof was red.
Rather imposing.

SHAKA IS AN ONLY CHILD FOR A LONG TIME.
At the crack of dawn he bathes in the river
while his mother watches him, hidden in a bush.
He rubs a substance into his young skin
to ward off Evil Spirits and acne.
A leader with a zit face would be a fiasco.
A leader with a squeaky little voice too.
Those mornings at the river, as he pours more water
over his back because he knows that his beloved
mother is watching him.
In the afternoons the game is on, his life is
made miserable (you can count on it) by the local boys and girls.
Example 1: they spit in his face.
Example 2: they kick his stomach and throw him into the stinging
nettles like a bag of rubbish.
Example 3: let's skip this one.
Example 4: they kick his ankles on the football pitch.
Example 5: they piss in his mouth (which someone holds open).
Example 6: they drag him into a brick hut
tie him up using chains and ropes
and leave him there for hours.
After another of those days he dreams
he has to cross a field full of black ping-pong balls.
When he begins to run the balls come shooting at him
one by one like bullets
a corrosive poison spreads through his body
paralysing his limbs.

Back to the river.
At full moon we see him there again.
He is probably not alone.
Lets himself sink into the glittering ink

and washes his hands and feet, his genitals
and rubs something into his forehead, everywhere
on all the soft shadow spots.

Shaka may be a bit strange but he is not unkind.
Loves hunting, birds and the magic violence of chess.
When a snake bites him, he unscrews its head
unpunished and sucks the poison from arm or leg or foot.
Is good at playing marbles and mental arithmetic.
When he thinks about fighting his body starts to itch.

Such a dear boy, vulnerable to the side effects of medicine
and then in no time, half-brothers are shooting up
from the ground like housing estates.
Father thinks Divide and Conquer, banishes his first-born
and his unlawful mistress.
How that hurts, *your own son*
the pain is indescribable, even to the tabloids.
Here too in this place, we'll skip this pain –
maybe another time, who knows.
Of course his father sends him a card now and then
but what good does that do.
In any case, Shaka and his mother live just
nine streets away.

Rejected by your own father
it is indeed no joke.
Little illegitimate scarecrow that you are.
Dead enough to live forever.
Look, here he comes at a run.
All muscles and suppleness.
Giant leaps towards an imaginary finish.
The crowds on the benches
and there, his mother, how miserable she looks.

Run, Shaka, run!

Stealthily I shove away the food bowl
there is a lot of food left.
All those wires cables ropes and chains
surely this is love, something I was desperately short of
I was old enough now.
Kept crazily chasing my own tail as it were
until I was so dizzy I had to lie down.
I've got dressed and undressed I wag my tail and pant
like I've just had a good hump, slap a mosquito on my cheek
already I can hear the first blackbirds – worryingly quiet
how quiet the television is, I get up cautiously
and want to shout something but I don't.
As though I were one of the family.
Tolerated, tamed, accustomed to this darkness through and through
and gift-wrap everywhere
all the lovely things I'd had.

I'm not comfortable I smell of cleaning products.
My teeth as pappy as wet cardboard, my skin porcelain.
Tap against it, you hear 'tick'.
My tongue clacks water water please
but clacking is not talking.
If only I knew more than I know now.
What I was waiting for, visitors, or something else.
So that I could fall into a deep sleep, wouldn't prowl.
Wandering along calmly, like a day out at the beach
only the sea was gone, I stared into a ghastly abyss
a rotting, bottomless pit –
and so I screamed for help
as though I were being shadowed by a horde of me's
as silent as stone.
Which was actually the case.
Me me me they bellowed in my ears.
Impossible to hear.
Back then I spoke a foreign language
neither heavenly nor natural.

SHAKA'S FAVOURITE SONGS.
'Eye of the Tiger' and 'I Was Made For Loving You'.
Sometimes he texts FUTURE to 3040 for a psychic reading.
The *Dark Knight* poster in his bedroom is decorated with yellow flowers
the superhero sucks at a bent ballpoint fag.
Underneath it written in black felt pen:
'Tell your men they work for me now. This is my city.'

The night before he takes a trip to the zoo
with his mother, Shaka dreams
that he is creeping stealthily through something that looks like a residential are
that still has to be completed – plastic pipes and concrete sheets
a lot of sand and steel tubes, pallets, some stones
the contours of a terraced house.
Somewhere here a lion is hiding –
the whole neighborhood shitting their pants with fear.
How daring he is, such a young fellow and so fearless.
Shaka's neighbours hide their faces in shame.
He rushes into a wreck and begins to roar unpleasantly.
The beast, afraid that it is surrounded by at least
a hundred warriors, backs into a small room
that will serve as a bathroom in a few months' time.
Makes itself small and smaller than a mouse, so small
that Shaka can crush it underfoot.
Which reminds us of Franz Kafka's 'A Litte Fable'.
Only Shaka doesn't eat mice, neither does he eat lions.
Later women will carry him around
the village on a shield
and so he awakens every morning into a world
that he grumpily provides with subtitles.
All those faces staring from the sidelines.

I skip along the street from left to right and back.
The music is playing pleasantly loudly
and not only inside my head.
My shadow is a super skinny strip, wafer-thin
my rucksack has the same shape same colour
the same dots as a squashed ladybird.
Houses, cars and dustbins all over the place
all of it flammable, all of it higgledy-piggledy.
There was a terrible storm but all around a heavenly light
pours over houses, gardens and roofs like a hot sauce.
This is romanticism from the olden days.
Before mankind started to stink
and was cuddled to death by gods and goddesses.
A vulture circles powerfully above all things –
strange, you never used to see those birds above these places.
Frozen from head to toe eyes shut
dreaming with the lights on as it were
I pick up a thick stick from the ground. Man
how long I take
such havoc too.

THE EFFERVESCENT TABLET.
Shaka's very own madeleine.
For headaches three times a day.
If still suffering after four days, consult your doctor.
Shaka doesn't have a high opinion of doctors.
Read too many books have too little knowledge.
One more effervescent tablet then.

And now a tablet the size of a manhole cover
splashes into the river where Shaka is swimming.
According to the stories, a snake shoots up out of all that wild churning
and din, even higher than a crane.
With the ears of a hare.
Those ears in particular make this anecdote outrageous.
But let's consider this image in all seriousness first.
The snake curling gracefully out of the river that effervesces and
gushes as if to fight an outrageous migraine.
Mother, hiding herself away in her usual spot
cannot believe her eyes.
That blazingly vital naked young man
she can call her son, newly unwrapped
and that cumbrous ancient creature that casts shadows across
the morning, reducing Shaka to a Lego figure.
She doesn't budge an inch.
Shaka and the snake look each other in the eye, keen and quick.
A kind of speed dating *avant la lettre*.
Then the creature rubs itself lovingly against Shaka's body
it's a very expensive scene, filled with megalomaniac special effects.
No freight ships no pleasure boats
no random cyclists on the banks – Shaka, snake and mother.

Pity that all of this takes place in the period
before the invention of sound.
Imagine all there is to hear!
A soft smacking sound, a happy gurgling
a tuneful humming, the abstract rustle in the rushes
and a voice-over announcing in a serious tone and with lots of violins
in the background that someday Shaka will rule.
Powerful little pill, Shaka thinks
once the monster has disappeared.
The headache has abated too.

In every dream there's a door (always mounted to the left).
You have to go through that door, once you're through you're safe.
Not dead, but safe.
Seems similar, the colours are different.
Look behind you and see no one
has followed you.
You see a forest, a field, perhaps a block of flats
or a parking garage.
Shaka sees it too.
Behind the cirrus clouds far in the distance
shaped like a brilliant ball:
the UFOs, always on the lurk.
But who believes in rumours here.

I'd been home maybe an hour
when I slipped out again.
Not long before the sun would set
I walked up the road to the woods behind the railway line
and the football pitches, carrying my homemade spear.
Its point a dreadful screech.
They said a dog had got out
some rare breed, jet black as a sermon
the froth that was on its jaws.
Barking to stay ahead of the darkness
I flitted after my shadow between the trees
until a solid curtain was ripped away.
Something lay there, half-buried under a few leaves and sand.
I raised my spear, took one step forward, froze.
As though I had suddenly forfeited the right to speak –
my T-shirt stuck to my chest
the prism of my skin was like a flickering dream.
For a second I emitted light
and then I was put out.

SHAKA'S MOTHER DREAMS OUT LOUD

My sparkling son walks onto the beach
pulls off his vest and shorts
his singing is outflanked by the breathing of the sea.
Full-on summer full-on blue skies.
A book on my lap there I sit in a red deckchair
at the waterline. *Passion in the Desert.*
When I was young I'd read Plath or a detective now and
then, I used to be forever young.
I see him frown he is fifteen feet away from me
seeming to direct the ocean with his hand.
Suddenly he's asking from very close by
Should I turn on the light? Reading in the dark
is bad for your eyes.
Laboriously I turn onto my side
who is knocking at the door but no
it's the surf kissing my feet
there he is again, standing up to his waist in the sea.
How he took cautious enjoyment as a little boy
when I sat in front of the mirror
pulling out my grey hairs with a pair of tweezers.
Shy smile on his lips.
Why didn't I pay more attention
how weary I am, how good this feels.
And all those footprints in the sand.

SHAKA AS A STRAY DOG AS A SAVIOUR.
Someone left flowers at the front door of his hut.
Like at a grave.
'May wolves devour him'
but the wolves avoid him:
seems he smells of something terrible.
Which keeps him alive.
Memories work overtime

and once again he rescues that girl from the jaws of a wolf.
Hears her shrieking like a dying light.
She's probably thinking I'm done for it has got me
lays me down nibbles at my feet
at my breasts at my legs, oh.
Then Shaka arrives, everything is shrouded in darkness
the wolf, the girl and the wild wild wood.
Now a fight breaks out like in a superhero comic.
Bold lettering, stars and exclamation marks.
Shaka throws his fists around crazily.
Sticks his spear into something then pulls it out again.
In a subsequent illustration he's sitting triumphantly atop the beast
as if on a two-seater sofa.
Then he boxes from left to right again
when he's had enough he presses pause
or runs away.
To a place where he can't even find himself.
There he keeps quiet and rests for a while.
Leaning on his broken spear.
In close up: his rage.

A few pages further and we see seven heads
skewered next to each other in a swamp.
Mouths wipe open.
Like hungering for honey
but the mouths gape for air.
A stench.
That's all there is.

WHEN DID IT START ALL THOSE VOICES INSIDE HIS HEAD.
A woman kneels in the white sand screaming.
Then another woman and another woman
not long after that a man –
this screaming is contagious, then another man
and then the dogs start up
in the back gardens, the gulls and the crows
in the dunes, the pigs and the ducks and the cats
and the monkeys and the giant parrot
and the giraffe and the dolphins in the bay.

Shaka thinks I've got a spear I am a muscle
I can kill anyone I want to kill.
Languid and listless he lies dozing in his hammock
in the cool shade of a tree.
The mass screaming in the background is like muzak
a buzzing nightmare.
His spanking new sidekick stands next to him
with a cool glass of ice-tea.
A kind of butler who tirelessly feeds Shaka's body
lubricates his spirit and overloads his aura with compliments.
Spotted in a brochure and then called up.

Of course this dear fellow has a sunny and a shady side.
'Can you hear that, all that sadness
this country is exhausted my friend
and you are predestined.' Shaka smiles satisfied
and watches the light playing in the leaves.

Faust made a pact with the devil.
Spain a pact with Malta (12-1).
Why not a pact with the perfect figment of your imagination?

'Be so kind as to bring me another cigarette.
And think of a name I can use to call for you.'

day(dream) #7,274

The lift is stuck the lights flash on and off.
Minutes cost time
I desperately need to concentrate, stay motionless.
The everyday soundtrack has gone without trace
only that monotonous buzzing remains.
The walls are dotted with flies, a black sticky mess
that would break free if I moved.
Order, I cry, order in court!
My eyes seek out the contours of a trapdoor
or something I could escape through, I dig upwards
until I'm outside again, newly born
everything echoes tremendously everything is still wet
my dicey brains have completely lost the plot
so wide I am I have to shout it out.
A shudder shoots through the cables –
strange my mobile isn't working.
And so hour after hour passes
I just hang here but I can't move back or forth
nothing but waiting
summoning up the courage.

ANYONE WHO HAS NOTHING TO LOSE CAN RAISE
THEIR HAND.

In a hasty sequence Shaka is mounted
with balsams, potions, his skin is injected
with antifreeze, his chest pumped up.
Others join up with their tails between their legs
but Shaka – it's a tune we all know by now.
See Charlemagne, see Pol Pot.
Caesar, Rambo.
I, II and III.
Who doesn't murder smothers, cried his mother's half-brother
and he should know.
Had his own butcher's and slaughtered the animals himself.
Until his own unexpected death.

Intoxication is a fast turning four-poster bed with many pillows.
The spear a narrow friend.

Without intoxication or assegaai Shaka is like Borges.
A blind poet.

I do the maths the whole neighbourhood seems paralysed.
The night smells of seasoned meat
the high whizzes through my veins.
I don't get up to put some food
something edible in my mouth
and to save the world from destruction.
I whistle quietly, my right eye a glass ball
I see more clearly with it than with my left eye
that looks and looks and looks and looks.
To think faster than light
but without any direction, sooner or later that will cause problems.
The first cracks shoot through the floor.
All the way from the kitchen wall to my feet –
an almost unbridgeable distance.
A blood-curdling sight.
That's all I want to say about it for now.

WHAT DOES BLOODLUST LOOK LIKE.
Maybe like a massive chunk of pure chocolate.
Sweet solidified darkness.

Shadows, whispering, footsteps, hissing.
Or in the words of Ovid, Book VIII:
'The gods take their seats.'
Cocaine white knuckles around the handle of his spear.
Unearthly lawlessness, not particularly photogenic.
Never again that jovial slap on the shoulder like
Hey, how you doing, man.
Never again Man you've lost weight
your hair looks great
you look so great with/without those glasses
in that blue shirt/with that rabbit fur headdress.

Shaka's voice sounds loud and anonymous after all that tinkering
with his body, a real radio voice and so
he returns to terrestrial life and mingles
in the daily bustle of the street, behaving
like a gentleman in the traffic.
For want of a more suitable term
we can speak of a Resurrection.
An unnoticed one, that's true.
No sign yet of debt, stress or insomnia
everything is going precisely as in your average myth.
What daylight cannot bear takes place in fields
or woods.

Often he who has been resurrected goes batshit crazy.
Shaka knows his way
with madness, a firm spear
is just like a penknife, *chop chop chop*.
Fighting a war or watching a football match in the stadium
it's all the same to Shaka
the same cheering and shouting, the same songs
the same hotdogs at half time
and no adverts no reporters.
So different from television where time
is stopped, slowed down, speeded up
in the repeat in which an opponent
is tricked by a clever decoy action.

The African summer shivers.
The heat hangs above the blood-drenched plain
like the dense smoke in a bustling kitchen.
Another match fought and won.
Minuscule flies that swarm in an open wound
and high in the heavens an eagle
drawing Olympic rings by way of a salute.
Our star player sits in the dressing room drenched in sweat.
Bottle of water in his hand, towel around his neck.
Replays the match in his head one more time.
A very expensive purchase but he's more than worth it.
A hero in the making and he can swim
like dolphins can swim.
With an appealing grin he pulls his weapon
from an opponent's throat, rewinds the film
and pulls his weapon from an opponent's
throat, rewinds
the film –

As clean as a pin I jump in and out of the shadow
of columns that are miles high, they seem to be made of stone.
The temple is missing an entrance I think or an exit
I was inside before I was even inside
that's how the mind works.
It's always the same old song, sorrow and sigh
like at the bottom of the sea
just waving weeds and darkness
there's almost nothing I can reach.
Not like with a man or animal.
Water, silence, running engines
the wind lying down in the grass
I hear everything muddled up.
The loveliest music in the world!
Not long ago I was called up by myself.
In the middle of the day, I recognized myself instantly
even though I didn't speak I shouted *You won't bloody believe this.*
There was a silly hiccupping laugh on the line —
before I knew it
the connection was cut off.

'it becomes visibly darker' — (day)dream #5,572

I stand shivering with cold what an infinitely large building.
I walked around the right-hand corner
then left then left again
through a gallery long enough for beautiful records.
I kept coming out somewhere different.
It is as if each new hour lasts longer everything in ruins.
Damp on the walls, columns, stairs, paintings
I see something glittering in my blind spot
something unimaginable like a sea of glass.
I shout out something randomly
just to hear a voice.
Where is my trail of pebbles to the *start*
where have my sins gone —
I should know
but I didn't pay much attention
now the day is almost over.

MATERNAL CONCERNS

What on earth is that son of mine up to.
How did he get so tough.
When did he start smoking.
And then those so-called friends of his.
Doesn't look at me when he speaks.
Actually that's a questions Why
doesn't he look at me anymore when he speaks?
Just like his father, all his clothes covered in blood every night.

'How was it?'
'Fine mum – what's for dinner?'
'Chicken, beans and rice. Chicken was on special.'
'*Cape Fear*'s on the telly, will you record it?'
'Are you going out?'
'Who knows.'

Apparently he meets his henchmen under the bridge over the river.
There are two of them, a fat one and a little one.
No one has ever spoken to those boys.
They have a smoke, I can smell it on his hair
Shaka buys a bag of hash, probably from that little one with the nose
who can see through secrets.
Really ugly fellow.
Shaka skips home as high as a kite –
I can just picture it, when he comes in
I pretend to be asleep on the sofa.
I simply call them his babysitters (he can't bear that)
Yin and Yang, his weather forecasters.
Must be big fans of Shaka's work.
Slime balls.
Well, I'm not, he knows that.

He talks in his sleep
sometimes he runs away from me, then I have to
go fetch him, exhausted I bring him in
and dab his forehead with a wet flannel
stroke his hair, rub his forehead

go to sleep now I sing softly
your mummy is keeping watch.

No waste anywhere not a trace.
Rock formations a river that rips the region in two
and colours it orange, boulders worn smooth
cold as chunks of water.
I think an hour ago I found the skull of a lamb
maybe a goat, a nose bone, gnawed clean.
That I remember this, unbelievable
I keep looking back, half human half tree.
It's as though I'm bent double from a laughing fit
stepping barefoot through a field of rats
death in my pocket.
I wanted to know what the world sounded like from very close up
but lumps of mineral clatter with abandonment
onto the zinc roofs of my cloudless dreams.
An unearthly roaring
it keeps me awake.
And soon that whole journey back.

AND SO SHAKA LEARNS TO LIE.
The same boy whom his mother knows all too well
has suddenly read the entire *Divine Comedy*.
And sure he can ride a bike, sure
he doesn't smoke, sure he'll finish his studies first.

A vigorous fire races in this afternoon hour across the expanses
driving his opponents straight
into his open arms, he stands waiting straddle-legged.
Stunt men are brought in – they don't actually burn.
Yin and Yang are cheerfully joining in the din
slashing around lustily, the little one and the fat one
slipping deafeningly out of their roles, as sharp as splinters of ice.

Shaka's fame spreads like a virus.
Scarves posters mugs pens badges –
the merchandise is in full swing.
But of course he's not interested in fame.

To burn or to drown, he wonders which is preferable.
Turns his back on the flaming spectacle
and pensively writes some ideas with his finger
in the oven-baked sand.
Totally oblivious.
Then reads what he's written.
Hastily rubs it all out.

The classic shoot-out.
And with so much competition too
it's bizarre, it makes my balls tingle.
I stand on one side and on the other side
there's me too, only the leaked version with a cold.
The albino smurf cut out of *The Smurfs*
and god knows what else.
Tension crackles like a fire in a paper factory.
I take another really good look –
how fat I've become, god almighty, solid I am not.
Like a dictator in formaldehyde.
Between us a boundless expanse, a concrete polar region.
Actually just a mixture of sand and grass
no larger than the back garden I used to lie in.
I see myself thinking but that's not my body
that's not me, I would never grope around my jacket pocket
for a mouth organ to play a foolish little tune on.

THE LITTLE ONE WITH THE NOSE.
A kind of cross between a human
and a dachshund, nothing but grimace.
If he's happy he rolls on his back, pedaling.
Spends the whole bloody day lying on Shaka's sofa watching soaps.
Empty crisp packets on the floor
and a few toppled bottles of beer.
Obediently feeds Shaka's fish.
Masturbates at least five times a day.

Then suddenly as alert as a waiter.
For example: Shaka
I can smell that someone wants to betray you, here's the address.
Or: Your father is dead
I thought I should tell you.

Shaka doesn't know whether to laugh or cry.
Finally he's broken free.
He only has to get past his oldest half-brother now.
A double feint and the crowds begins to cheer.
Another feint and the cheering surges.
There's the goal, the keeper is already lying on the ground.

Shaka has two goldfish.
Calls them One and Two.
Strings of semen float through the aquarium
like final exhalations.

Three two one I kick some earth into the grave
I'm not very focused.
I've been digging all night, screaming, chipping away
I'm so exhausted I can hear the ocean.
That hoarse magnificent power station.
I desperately need a pee
I fiddle secretly with the marbles in my trouser pocket.
The coffin is brown and smooth, just a standard coffin.
I'm supposed to get a move on now
to honour, to serve
but it's as if I cannot think ahead
or I'm about to collapse.
I'm standing here pretty much on my own
it's not even a beautiful radiant day.
Soon I will set off on foot again –
I can already find the path leading back to the entrance
without any help.
Pretty clever
it's a real maze here.

DEAR ME,

You ask whether I'm still plagued by dreams about the days after my death.
Yes I am, but they're cheerful!
Men, women, infants and old people, lunatics and criminals no one has a clue what to do.
Hoarse from weeping people shuffle across the streets to publicly protest against my passing away.
All that noise and what revulsion too.
And everything live on air!
Owls, magpies, sparrows, crows hide in the trees that are losing too many leaves, running rivers
cease running, lions, elephants, pelicans kneel in the sand to pray for my soul's rest.
Mountains overcome by pity reluctantly creep closer a mass of civilians and soldiers
stand hysterical along the route and fine snow is constantly falling, left alone by the
north wind.
Come to think of it, it's more of a prediction than a dream.
For instance I don't appear in it myself.
The coffin is empty, only my voice can be clearly heard.
I do know that I smile at all of this – all that love, yes, I approve!
You'll understand that I can't wait until this happens.

Apart from that everything is hunky-dory. You've probably already heard that.
Yours, S.

(day)dream #4,952

A solitary sheep grazes on the other side of the river.
I can hear it shuffling around and sniffing like an old man
I'm so stuck on my sound
I stare and stare until I can no longer see it.
I walk towards the water as though on command.
Like a hunter off to see what damage his shot has caused
while he feels surrounded on every side
and the rain is pounding on the roof of his hunting lodge
not far away – not a single light is burning there
the door is open a chink.
A horrific stench slams into your face
when you step inside, I stood there reeling
like a heaving ship.
What was I doing there.
Distraught I fled the lodge
into the woods where they found me
drenched
to the skin.

ATTEMPT AT AN INTERVIEW

'Take a seat – had a good journey?'

'Shaka can't complain.'

'Did you pick up on anything of the local folklore –
do you mind if I use the informal?'

'I only just got here, this is my first interview today.
I didn't come across much to see.
But I've almost finished the *Lonely Planet* © guide.'

'Excellent name for a travel guide!
I'll turn it on now, alright? First question
What question have you been asked the most often?'

'Whether I'm exactly the same in real life.'

'Well?'

'Depends what you consider the Past tense
but it would be hard to deny everything, no
there's certainly a grain of truth in there.'

'A reader's question, something lots of readers wonder about.
What have you actually done for the world – oh, Shaka
you're not allowed to smoke here, I'm afraid.'

'What's this man doing next to my chair?'

'He's the interpreter for the deaf.'

'The deaf? But isn't this for a newspaper?'

'Just a precaution.'

'You're kidding me?'

'He's really an excellent interpreter.'

'Really? Well let's see if he can do this gesture!'

I don't want to see another attraction
my skin is as dry as a raisin.
Dirty from the outside air and all the tourism.
I don't want to sleep with the lights off
I don't want to sleep with the lights on
it's not peak season yet I hear water running
children's voices, crackling wood
I'm given instructions like at home.
Someone comes running up to me from a long way away, frantic
just like me and left behind.
I don't look in the mirror otherwise I'll break loose
I'm almost breathless from listening.
A small wardrobe, a bed, a table and two chairs.
That's all there is.
I said I'd like a two person room please.
A joke occurred to me –
must have been the nerves
I was given a key
and took the lift upstairs.

SHAKA FINALLY FINDS THE LOVE OF HIS LIFE
in one of his mother's fashion magazines.
Those eyes and that small chin, those cheekbones!
Calls her N, how should he describe her?
Like an evening stroll after a magical film.
Like a drive in a dilapidated Beetle
between rocky mountains, meandering along a glassy stream
and suddenly the sun breaks through
the sunlight breaks through the air, far below
the valley where he will spend the night.
N! Like an abrupt taste that explodes in your mouth
heavy rain at the height of summer.
As addictive as a football game.
His biographer complains of hackneyed imagery.
Never mind as long as it works, Shaka thinks.
Who crushes so guilelessly but cannot dance.
Who keeps treading on his partner's toes.
Has no idea how to offer a drink
how to kiss with your whole mouth.
As a young boy he was often teased about love.
'Fat Babette is shagging Shaka'
and 'Shaka = Nerd' in giant letters
on the side wall of the corner shop.
Bitter, he ran home, hid himself away
in his bedroom and didn't come out for days.

He concentrates on sharpening the point of his spear
and wonders whether N knows of his existence.
Whether in her dreams he rescues her from the flames
and whether she sprays a little perfume between her breasts
while looking at his photo, leaves the dinner to burn
and disguises her imperfections with make-up

while humming 'They can't take that away from me'.
About four times a week and
crazy with longing he heads towards
the red-lit backstreets of the village.
He stays there until he is completely broke.
Long after midnight he's still roaming the streets.
Living from minute to minute
on his way to more and still more life.

I fill my lungs with evening air
the door falls smoothly shut.
All that chatter, the plurality is lost
I button up my coat, step onto the pavement.
Ready for my dive into immortality.
I screwed above my station, all the things promised to me
it wasn't much, my hands sought something to hold on to
I thought This is your chance, hurry up you idiot.
The fog horn blows a wet base note
into my inner ear – this must be over soon.
What am I without alibi, a butcher without a knife
an insignificant animal, a hedgehog that curls up
and rolls down the street, going faster and faster
until its small mass is nothing but noise and speed
and it shoots straight at its goal
more or less.

A beautiful fire spreads through the dunes
all the smoke drifts towards the sea.
The fields and the poorly-lit villages.
I followed the river until I saw something flickering
at first I thought it was fireworks, I climbed and climbed
then I was at the top.
I threw everything I could grab into the flames
lusty with feckless desire.
The smell of smoke in my clothes, in my hair
turns my toil into a heroic deed
for all I know the enemy is watching.
If I had to describe the heat I'd whisper
if anyone looked for me in this life I'd be nowhere to be found –
no narrative, no drama
just a trace of ashes on charred grass
and smouldering remains.
Of what
it was no longer possible to make out.

IN THESE PLEASANT OLD-FASHIONED DAYS
an experienced messenger is a bonus.
More careful than just a phone call.
Tell so and so that the meeting will start at such and such a time.
Messenger on the way, four days of privation.
A meeting? Sure, but I can't make that particular day.
Tell them that I'm available at such and such a time
only a week later.
Question and answer take miles
and lots of messengers, the broken ones exchanged for fit and fresh.
And so after a lot of running, the news arrives that Shaka
will succeed the dead leader.
The questions during the press conference are mainly
of a rhetorical nature.
Are you happy now, are you stronger, cleverer, tougher than the rest.
Have you already paid your assistants.

His butler and the fat one and the little one with the nose.
Nagging him like a mother.
Don't forget to do something with your spear
at least once a day; a day without death
is a day not lived — you can take this literally.

Now just his father's blessing.
Stars and famous people often get
the prettiest women, drive the most expensive cars
live in the biggest houses with a swimming pool and a boat
and a holiday home at the seaside to top it off.
Shaka arrives at the cemetery on horseback.
Accompanied by five stunning virgins.
Although the sources contradict each other on this point.
He wisely keeps on his sunglasses.

This is how he'll be pictured in the newspapers later.
Sand blows around the plain, somewhere sorrow is simmering.
Now my sidekick is going to talk to the gravestone
that'll be funny – the loony.
That's what you get from an alcohol problem plus poverty.
They drive you totally bananas.

Tapping the blessings from a block of granite
is an entire ceremony.
That his dad suddenly begins to speak!
In a language understood by nobody!
What a story this will make.

(day)dream #4,260

I nimbly crawl through the bushes to the main road.
My oxygen mask fits perfectly
the earth seems flat I'm lying so low.
I push a branch away from my face
the crossroads have been cleared, fenced off.
The day started imperceptibly as though I didn't exist.
I practiced my smile in the mirror
and laughed and laughed until my smile was chiseled.
People point and shout, an angry prayer
I feel no guilt exactly like a machine.
Only my own breathing, I can only hear my own breathing.
When I lie on my back and look up
I gauge a depth that is disconcerting
just like the force with which I stick to the world.
If I let go I fall and I fall and fall
towards the darkness and trillions of stars
until I keep on falling.

SOMEWHERE IN AFRICA'S SOUTHERN TERRITORIES
a spectacular coronation is being prepared.
Squares are being swept, journalists are being
sent inland, someone is composing
a song for the king, someone is making special mugs
with a portrait of Shaka on them, roaring with laughter.
Or with a close up of his hand clutching a spear.
Or with an UFO – Shaka's logo.

A brilliant war is fought at top speed
totally high Shaka lashes out around him.
Straight back, tall and supple, beautiful in his ugliness.
It's a popular theory: power lends beauty.
Shaka's mouth opens and closes
but nobody hears him scream.
On film it looks peculiar.
Lots of dust, lots of chaos, lots of extras
who can't help looking into the camera
even though the director warned them specifically.
The lens focusses on Shaka's hands
on his eyes, his teeth, his crotch.
Maybe N is drunk with admiration
right now.
And everyone sees something different.
The boy playing with blocks sees a hero
the soldier a comrade
the whore a regular customer.
History recognizes the devil in disguise.
The animal a clever hunter.
Death a supplier.

Today I wasn't so bad
and all the world languages I spoke!
How recently I danced blind drunk
with a woman who said moist things
close to my ear. Well well. But around dusk
suddenly I shot upright like an accusation
knife in hand, totally sober now
as though I were protecting someone
and seeking revenge at the same time.
Small birds raced low over my brick, wood and zinc
neighbourhood and something in me said *Go on*
finish it off – where could I go
it was as if I were on an island.
An island is nothing but a pocket hunting ground
surrounded by Delft blue water
if it's tropical, with palm trees and hotels
and on the back some lines for name and address
and at the bottom *It's really beautiful here*
the people are very friendly and so normal
take care, see you soon, love –

SMALL SELECTION OF THE CORONATION'S LOGISTICS

Present are around three hundred musicians.
Shaka's throne has been restored especially for this day.
Four kilometres of fabric has been used for the banners.
Ten thousand imported flowers bake in the sun.
There's a total ban on advertising.
More than five thousand police are keeping an eye on the crowds.
Two hundred events are taking place including
seven public executions and eight dance parties.
Protesting and urinating in public are punishable with the death penalty.
The coronation is entirely at the expense of the government.

I was standing about here when someone slapped my face
a serious blow, I rolled over and was a thing.
I bit out uncontrollably and missed
as though I'd been washed up on a burning beach.
Swans bobbed away on the waves
as listless as death, whatever still moved was moving in its sleep.
And then and then
I still remember that I remained lying down and didn't run away, plastered
right through the soft lining of the night.
That sounds dopey, I pick up a leaf from the ground
shaped like a duck's foot, the whole park is full of them
the trees I estimate at least thirty metres high
very different from the trees back home.
I spit, and again
I can't get rid of the strange taste.
Horrible splinters in my hands
all the streetlamps are burning –
I can tell I've been away for a long time
it's not that dark.

AN INEXPLICABLE HOBBY

Shaka's UFOs don't come
from an unworldly world.
Not from a leaking archive of
planets, stars, weather balloons and meteors.
If they show themselves it's in the form of light effects
in the sky, a fiery noise
like a collapsing block of flats.
A noise that often coincides with prayer.
Sometimes they take the form of a snake
that hangs around for days.

Shaka begins to save up the appearances
and shoots roll after roll of film.
When he's washing himself in the river one morning
a triangular object lands in the middle of the water.
As wary as a dip pen on thin paper.
After a while a shining staircase slides down.
Or take that time when one of Shaka's bulls went missing.
After a long search he comes across a clearing
in the woods and sees a number of things
a) a strange shining ball
b) a handful of humanoids
c) his favourite bull, its stomach cut open, no trace of blood.
Shaka still doesn't know why he first froze
and then launched a furious attack a second later.
As though someone had flipped a switch.
His room is full of colourful pieces of evidence.
A vertical crater like an upright fish
whose midriff can swell and shrink back.
Gnome-like beings without ears or eyes
with dark blue faces, as transparent as glass.

The last time Shaka saw something unusual
was when he was just driving around.
A technically incorrect object hung
above an area of smoky rock.
Located in the future many days' travel from here.
A desperate area.
Without plants without depth without animals.
Once he got home Shaka slept like a log.
A very heavy one.
A sleep which lasted, it's said
from then onwards.

day(dream) #3,637

I've turned on the windscreen wipers
my brown skin is dark brown from all the summer days.
Villages, craters, reserves, everything glides past.
As though I'm rushing through a tunnel with wet cement
and at the end of it that famous light and clear sounds.
Only there is no tunnel, I can't describe it
not even now I'm asleep, not even now I'm not asleep.
And I stiffen, I can't help it, it just happens –
a plank made of flesh, I shudder at the thought
like a rat, my tail a fat worm and there
a tomcat lurking there just at the edge
of my intellectual ability.
Come out the creature cries I can see you.
At this point I used to jerk awake
bathed in sweat
now I can laugh about it, I screech
with pleasure as though on an eternal holiday
see me screeching here.

Sweat pours down my back suddenly I've lost my script.
I stand here messing around with a map
it seems like an eternity.
Bare trees, tidy streets, shutters closed
but all the houses are inhabited.
At least that's what I heard.
I leave the engine running just in case.
My car is made of stainless steel but where I go I go in peace.
The day went by without stopovers, with potholes
and mist, traffic jams, arid brush, nothing but sand
and all of it without stars without light.
As though I were wandering through my own brain
as though I had drowned in a sea of mercury —
perhaps I'm not reading the map right.
It's freezing cold out here.
Reeling with lightness I tread on a dog, I think
something hairy, it lies there without moving.
If only someone would speak to me, someone who could understand me.
I mean, it's already evening
I think I should have gone left there
at that playground
only it's a dead end street.

THE KING IS DEAD LONG LIVE THE KING.
Shaka's father, stabbed in the back but 'King Shaka'
sounds a lot better than just 'Shaka'.
Only a coward attacks from behind – that's how
Jesse James died too, though accompanied by film music.
The old leader fell in total anonymity.
Like a leaf from a tree among other leaves.

War is a devilish brew of sweat
testosterone and bad breath, there's not
a lot to be gained: a bit of land, some cattle, that's all.
Nevertheless Shaka's men put on an almost
perfect fight today: test-driving their new weapon.
A small spear, not to be thrown from a distance
but to use for short powerful stabs.
Shaka should put a patent on it.
An hour later the countryside is strewn
with more than a thousand lifeless beings.

The new king stands atop the hillside
like a communist statue.
Checking to see if anyone is still moving, if he
can spot a half-brother or an uncle in this silent chaos.
His shield raised above his head.
Every thought frozen.

I have put aside my binoculars
the evening paper lies crumpled in a corner like a dead bird.
The wind chased through the streets
I sang along out loud, I'm on edge
a timebomb without a clock.
In a future life I unbuttoned my shirt
took off my trousers
emptied my glass.
As though I were being controlled by a merciful computer.
I lay there a while before I fell asleep
the grinding of my teeth sounded peaceful
like the rusty turning of the earth.
Bravely I stood on an escalator down to the sea
and soon after that I sailed diagonally on the wind –
there I went, there I went
I was firmly embraced
I had jaw pain from smiling.
Water, friction, oxygen.
Something imaginary to honour.
In those days it was all so simple.

DELICIOUS!

In the shower.
On the table.
On the washing machine.
That shakes and vibrates and roars.
Under the table.
In the lift.
Under the asphalt.
On the bench.
In front of the window.
While playing chess.
In the lab.
In the public toilets.
In the train and at the office.
In the darkroom.
On the beach.
And in the sea.
Or up a mountain.
In the winter.
In the car.
In the fruit basket.
In the fridge.
In the kitchen.
Among the cast-offs.
In the garden.
Before going to sleep.
In the sauna.
During swimming.
While doing the dishes.
In the fitting room.
In the cinema.
And yes, in bed.

Something is squashed the skid marks look about fifteen feet long.
Maybe a giant berry, a magpie or a fox
just like in my animal book with pictures
as small as keyholes.
The whole thing locks mechanically
the stench of piss and burning rubber
plastic light cuts through the windows.
I press my head against the glass
a snorting horse in a cramped boiling horsebox.
I have forgotten how many days pass before I climb out
the air is fresh as I kneel down
and inspect the damage
to my left and right the lashing lyricism of fields of flowers –
I see only a big black stain.
What should I do now.
Gradually my hand begins to stroke that stain
strong and firm until the keening stops.
All in all a stupid gesture.
It's beautiful here by the way, quiet too
I'd never really noticed.

day(dream) #2,608

I'm playing chess against the computer I'm in check.
My right arm is in plaster
there's a bell around my neck so that people can hear me.
A wonderful game it was, for a few hours
my life did not belong to me nor to science.
As though I were skipping rope on the moon.
Always a new catwalk, always the same suit.
Of course I could shout out well done, computer
in a dented voice, I delay things a little.
As though I could set off a war
by merely getting to my feet.
I look at my black king again on e8.
The silence glistens like a lump of crystal
that makes patterns on the ceiling and the walls.
I should paint the place sometime –
cracks, mould, dirt, but at night
it's not very visible.

THE SHORT SPEAR – AN INTRODUCTION VIDEO

One holds up the shield, preferably to the left of the face. Not too low, this tires the arms. Not too high, one doesn't see anything then. One takes the short spear in one's right hand and grasps it firmly around the middle. If one drops it, one is lost. Now one thrusts in short, hard stabs, remembering to keep the shield nicely upright. As one stabs with the right, one takes a step forward with the left leg. Pay attention to the left leg. Then back again right away. Repeat at least nine times. A short stab forward and then a step back. Stab forwards step back. If one invents a rhythm to accompany this as though training at the gym then it must be as though one is stabbing but doesn't quite dare. That's how quickly one withdraws the spear. It resembles fighting with a sword (one hand on the handle, the other halfway along the blade). Without a suit of armour of course and the short spear is never waved around. Control is of great importance since one has limited access to the opponent's vital parts. There are three techniques for the short spear and only two positions. Learn first to carry out an attack from the basic position. Even an amateur can learn this technique. Don't forget to practice for speed. Try it at home or in the garden and sign up. Volunteers will be subjected to a strict examination. We will test your sight and your urine and your hearing or no wait, your heart. Interested in the selection process? Read the brochure 'Trial and Selection'. We look forward to hearing from you and wish you good luck.

The weather outside is rotten, miserable and wet.
Everything is smeared with blood, my trousers my shirt my glass.
I wanted to order something
talk about something before I forgot it all again.
For example that every morning
I stand face to face with my spitting image
a gloomy ocean with the odd small boat
or a drowning person who waves as though he's unexpectedly on TV.
Or that I was walking through the woods, that was today
less than a mile from here.
I had tools with me, a hammer and a saw
a bit of tape and for a moment it was as though I'd get lost —
all those hills, all that water
then that density of branches and that crackling canopy of leaves
in a delirium the scarce light in long thin tracks.
I took a good look around but I really was alone
as man as animal as thing
I wasn't dreaming, on the contrary.
I was there, now I'm here.

THE CAUSE OF THE WET STENCH THAT HAS BEEN
SPREADING SINCE MONDAY MORNING HAS BEEN
FOUND. AFTER HOURS OF SEARCHING AND
MEASUREMENTS THE SOURCE WAS TRACED.
A CONCLUSION HAS BEEN MADE: THERE IS AN
OUTBREAK OF DEATH IN THE COUNTRY.

With this hydrogen sulfide is released.
The smog is carried far across the country's borders
by the southerly wind.
By now it has been smelled at sea and unfortunately
has proved fatal to many old people and small children.

SHAKA'S BRIEF FLIRTATION WITH ROMANCE

One day he appeared at her door like an apparition.
It must have been his first and last attempt.
Bunch of flowers in his hand, some roses and chrysanths
clean smoke blowing out of the smoke machine behind him
and the universe dangling on ropes
consciously apolitical and shining.
It had cost a pretty penny, some serious logistics
and bloodshed, but his anticipatory pleasure
set its sights on the spectacle in her bed.
If anyone had tried to pull one over on him
at that moment, he would have stood his ground.
Knocked and knocked again and then again.
After some discussion it turned out
he was at the wrong house!
Laughing in disbelief, locals slid
down from the trees, windows were closed again
the ladies from the drum band also made an about turn.
Silently he was led off
a decrepit barge in an immense canal
and people forgot about the whole business so that it
would never ever happen again.

Something has gone wrong.
I hang like shot game catching copious amounts of wind
high above a city.
Office glass everywhere, the blood slowly leaves my arms.
Something burning in the distance, a pack of dogs
bark angrily on the asphalt down below
helicopters hover out of sight rattling like egg whips.
Up to now, I'd always done my own stunts.
I utter a few screams that aren't in the script
that I fought evil with evil
evil was like a cockroach.
I always turned up when needed
before wandering off triumphantly into the future during
the closing scenes
my deeds and misdeeds forgiven and forgotten –
I never shot my mouth off
I'd rather let go.

SHAKA READS THROUGH THE SPORTS RESULTS.
He had the photos from his childhood burned.
Now all he needs is a name for his people.
History describes him as frigid.
Love is transaction, clean hands.
Now that he's moved up might N want to share her life with him?
Sex before a war – there are various theories about that.

Power is like a rare china ornament.
Once you finally own it what can you do with it –
it breaks so easily in two
his empire is large, his empire needs to be bigger, so back
to the cornerstone of every myth: the Sacrifice.

Shaka signs a declaration.
The sacrifice begins and ends with one letter.
The n for N.
No, that's not a joke.
But Shaka isn't laughing.
Not at all in fact.

It had cooled down.
On my minuscule balcony
I didn't stand a chance against the hubbub
so before going to sleep I cast down the anchor
from the second floor which was fixed to the outside wall
by a heavy chain.
With a muffled splat it disappeared into the ground.
A gaggle of geese drifted around in the grass beneath my flat
like a drunkard's prayer.
I'd bet on them being geese – cackling
white-grey splodges.
Not long after midnight half awake
and overcome by blindness
I was drawn towards the window that was now open, just caught
a glimpse of the village vanishing into the horizon.
The chain the anchor had been fixed to
swung wildly back and forth.
I closed the window as quietly as I could
not wanting to make a noise, went
back to bed.

AFTER DINNER SHAKA DRIFTS OFF IN FRONT OF THE TELEVISION

'Normally I'd introduce the contestants to you first
today there's only one contestant.'

'...'

'Who are you, what do you do, where are you from.'

'...'

'Shaka, can you hear me, would the technician
sort out his microphone please.
I see you're black, where are you from.'

'I'm not black, take a better look.'

'Well, yeah, black... Not from here in any case.
What do you do for a living?'

'I paint sometimes, I like to play chess. Sometimes I move a mountain.'

'Let's start. Press the button if you think
you know the answer, no... yes, that one.
If you give an incorrect answer
your points will go to your opponent.
Given we don't have one today
the points will be wiped out.
There it is, our wipe-out machine.
Solid and classic, a wondrous machine.
Made in Japan.
Good luck, you can start now!'

Concentrate, first word, five letters.
Begins with a P ends with a R.'

'Power.'

'No, that's wrong, ball 38, a word with an S
ends with an R, five letters.'

'Spear.'

'What a shame, Shaka, I'm going to have to count that as a wrong answer.
You can ask an audience member for help, no – you're shaking your head.
Okay, the bonus letter then, the Z, five letters, oh, a tricky one.'

'Power.'

'I'm looking at the jury.
I said I'm looking at the jury.
No, sorry Shaka.'

'...'

'Right, to whom can we attribute this famous saying:
To write poetry after Auschwitz is barbaric. Was it
a) Jean-Paul Sartre
b) Andy Warhol
c) Theodor Ludwig Wiesengrund Adorno
or d) Primo Levi?'

'e)...?'

'For 30 points, Shaka, no, 50 even – a, b, c or d.'

'I'm in the dark here.'

'Al Pacino, *Scent of a Woman*.'

'Originality is not my strong point.
Women neither, for that matter, can I call my sidekick?'

'The phone line has been sabotaged.'

'...'

'There's war everywhere, Shaka, death and decay.
Smoldering ruins – you know the images.'

'I'll come back to that later.'

'Perhaps you'll do better at this one.
Which ingredient does not belong in a *bobotie*?
a) minced beef
b) milk
c) leek
or d) curry powder
For 10 points.
Minced beef, milk, leek, curry powder.'

'It must be "leek" I think, answer c.
Yes, I'll go for "leek".'

'Fan-tas-tic! Moving on quickly to the next question
Which female singer had a hit in the 1980s
with the song *J'aime j'aime la vie*?'

'Let me think.'

'*J'aime j'aime la vie*.'
For 20 points.
Ball 79.'

'Nena?'

'Nena's German. Never heard of *J'aime j'aime la vie*?
Shaka, are you also in love with life?'

'I love playing chess, I pl–'

'Surely you'll know this one, complete the sentence
We shall fight dot dot dot.
We shall fight dot, dot, dot.'

'I've never been much of a fan of Churchill's poetry.
Pumped-up journalist. A noxious dictator who onl–'

'But the answer, what's the answer?'

'On the beaches.'

'Almost.'

'On the beaches.'

'No. Almost right.'

'On the beaches.'

'Last chance.'

'I give up.'

'Almost right, I said.'

'I give up, I said.'

'Jury?... No, sorry Shaka, on to the next one.
What sleeps in a lair...
what sleeps in a lair.
Not a sound from the audience, please.
For 100 points.'

'Trick question?'

'No, Shaka, it's not a trick question.'

'Is that a trick question, I ask sternly, I don't like trick questions.
Makes my blood boil, the consequences can't be foreseen.
That's an historical fact.'

'I know, I understand. Sorry. No, not a trick question.'

'This.
Is.
A.
Trick.
Question.'

'Hmm. Maybe we should just count that one right – you haven't
got a problem with syllables that's for sure. I'll just glance at the
jury... jury, where's the jury... wait, Shaka. Hey...! Would the
audience sit down, where's the audience? Guys, you can't do that,
come on folks, where have those locusts come from all of a sudden,
I'm looking at the jury, I said Can somebody just come take a look,
bloody hell, somebody, hey... guys, turn off that thing wait, wake
up wake up, Shaka! King Shaka!
Wake up.
Hey, wake up!'

'curfew' — day(dream) #1,263

Snow blocks the streets the cat sits in the window.
Black flowers in a black vase.
Black streamers and balloons.
A tin crown upon my head
in my memory faces and faces
I never forget a face.
I just ate cake and more cake
from early in the morning 'til late at night
as though I had to celebrate something urgently.
As though I'd brought about some kind of miracle.
Although I was no angel.
I've had it up to here with all the moaning and barking
in the room next door, I really don't want to hear it.
Deer in the kitchen, elephants in the park
and fireworks and valleys, what else can I make up.
I want to go home, I only came to take a look.
Check up on things, it's like a fridge in here –
that's how it goes, hot air rises, cold air
sticks around.

ENEMIES BLEND IN WITH SHAKA'S PEOPLE LIKE
PICKPOCKETS IN A CROWD.
If he looks to the left he sees oceans quake.
If he looks to the right he sees the mountains smile.
If he looks up he sees the stars winking at him
but he is itching himself in places it can't itch
and more and more often he talks to himself.
If his smile clouds over so does the sky
mist descends on his kingdom and screams ring out, somewhere.
Where is N when you need her, a soothing word
would make a difference – *Shaka, darling, take it easy.*
But N is nowhere to be seen and she doesn't have any lines yet
maybe the odd word here and there
but she is poorly lit and made of cheap paper.

The headquarters are located where two rivers intersect.
With shops, subjects and some animals.
A street plan made of straight lines and a square
in the middle like a stamp.
A leader without a square is no leader.
His decorative ornaments of the female gender
live a stone's throw away, they make a racket
praising his cock, his agility, his hands
while he boldly strolls around in his tiger print
suit which makes him seem taller.
His people look like a machine, a fluid manoeuvre.
Professionalisation is the magic word.

Soldiers need to be able to kill with one slash
and use their tongues politely.
Be able to dance, sing, tell jokes

and play an early form of football.
Be as silent as the grave except about war.
Don't speak with their mouths full or to a lady.

Security is notched up a level too.
A fence, inside it another fence
then one final fence
a whole set of passwords
only then will you find yourself face to face with Shaka.

But where is Shaka?

A TERRIBLE DANCER, A DOWN-AND-OUT,
A SHEPHERD BOY, A BORN LEADER, A PRETTY
GOOD LEFT-WINGER, A MILLIONAIRE, A LIAR,
A VILLAGE IDIOT, A CHAUVINIST, A DICTATOR,
A DEAF MUTE, A VISIONARY AND AN ASYLUM-
SEEKER STAGGER INTO THE PUB TOGETHER.

Barman, 'So, Shaka, what will it be?'

'self-portrait as Saint Nicholas' – day(dream) #1,015

Loud banging on the door.
If it wasn't me
I'd dive behind the curtains screaming.
I came by train – my horse died
the boat sank, I crawl onto the roofs, spent.
If I do speak, I speak ten to the dozen
if I hold my tongue I'm very old
full of lies and deceit
no longer afraid to shake God's hand.
When it's my turn to go
I pull on my ordinary clothes, buy a first class single
slumber on the way like a guard
step out on a windswept platform
and shuffle incognito,
the sunlight on my neck,
along a sandy path, dead normal.
How well I recognise everything here
I'm already walking faster than just now
until, as elated as a small child
I break into a run.

AN EXCLUSIVE INTERVIEW WITH ONE OF SHAKA'S FOOTSOLDIERS

A sticky Friday afternoon.
On the terrace of Café Sizobonana, Sipo's eyes shine
then he looks troubled again.
A desolate young man.
Smokes non-stop, looks over his shoulder constantly.
Doesn't have much time.

'But you work for a murderer?'

'Those aren't my words.
This is my fate as a soldier, I don't give a damn about politics.
Shaka's just a normal, friendly man.
He likes playing chess, driving and fishing.
Sometimes he gives us the afternoon off.'

'He's popular with the ladies?'

'He gets a lot of fan mail from men too.
Sometimes we'll play a game of football on the battlefield.
He watches us, almost moved
sometimes a woman will stalk him
but the stuff about those sex orgies is bullshit.
Shaka's a good boss.
After a day of fighting he often buys a round.'

'You're taken care of properly?'

'I studied Marxism.'

'But all that bloodlust?'

'I don't want to defend myself, of course
there's a death or two, but that's because there's a war on!'

'What does your average day look like?'

'We get up at four when the world is cold and wise.
First a cup of coffee then we sharpen
the weapons, get our kit together
and go off in search, into the future.
Don't get me wrong, you can lose yourself completely there
we always come across new terrain.
In the evenings we're quiet, after a successful day
we play snakes and ladders or argue about football,
about women, there's always alcohol and smokes.
Until Shaka says goodnight, then we crawl into our beds
kind of large socks made from agricultural plastic.'

'You don't have any doubts?'

'No comment.'

'You must all see the news?'

'We don't read the papers here.
Sometimes I'm allowed to call home
but not for too long because war
requires discipline.'

'Rumour has it that you were punished.'

'Shaka's a good boss, no comment.
Any enemies wanting to join our people
will find a warm family here.
Anyone who flees or turns away in fear – well
we are and remain a fighting machine.'

'Explain that.'

'I don't have to defend myself
I don't come from another planet, this is my fate as a soldier.
If you want to kill someone in battle
don't cut his windpipe but go for his neck arteries.
That's a tip I can give you for free
I've had more than enough of this chitchat.
Nothing ventured nothing gained.
With the best will in the world you can't make more of it than that.'

I've moved a bit further along
maybe I'll get a bite now.
A gull glides diagonally above my head
while the rubbish of days sloshes against the quay: cans, bags, fish
everything that floats a bit, I have to keep
looking for my float.
Thunder rolls in from the east.
There the river curves to the left
the sky's canopy is black with clouds.
As though the world has already gone up in smoke
as if everything I see already belongs to the past.
It wouldn't surprise me.
Say I jumped down and walked right across the water
to all those houses on the other side
totally dated, just like in the brochure.
Where all those people are standing staring
at something taking place behind me –
I could get there within a couple of minutes.
Not that I'm impatient
but this isn't going to be a success
in fact I'm standing here like a fool.

FOR A LONG TIME SHAKA STARES SILENTLY
INTO THE CAMERA.
Behind him the tense faces
of his butler and the fat one and the little one with the nose.
Nothing to fear from the people
the people are calm and peace-loving this morning.
Wouldn't want to change places with any other people.
From the speakers comes the question of
whether he's ready to start, *Are you ready.*
N, or a glorious future – think very carefully.

The end, of N – we can be brief about it.
Sits in her hut reading *To Kill A Mockingbird.*
Brown and blushing as though she's pregnant
her eyes as clear as a mathematical formula.
Shaka thinks of the temptation
of her juicy lips, sees himself soundlessly
going up to her, stabbing her in the side
from behind, as though embracing her.
After which she deflates and lies down very quietly
on the ground and mutters, I see... a star.
Shaka doesn't hear her but with these words
N joins a list of famous names.
John Lennon: 'I'm shot.'
Goethe: 'More light!'
Jean-Paul Sartre: 'I've failed.'
Stan Laurel: 'I'd rather be skiing.'
Princess Diana: 'My god, what's happened.'
Henrik Ibsen: 'On the contrary.'

Shaka steps back perplexed

and flees the hut, then the street, then the village.
As he's standing resting next to a tree
a massive roar rushes at great speed across the fields
towards him, as though a million
zips are being closed at the same time.
For a few minutes all Shaka can hear is
a high-pitched bleep in his ear.
There is no world left
to conquer.

Simplicity strikes in one fell swoop
I was breathing and then I wasn't.
As though I was trapped in a revolving door
could see in could see out.
I like to come here, there used to be a clump of trees over there
and nothing else except colour and silence.
If a story is re-told enough times
its contents naturally evaporate
what is left of it, earth, stones, roots, chalk
and lighting so cruel it makes me laugh.
As though I'm dancing without moving.
The mountains, the valley, the village full of tourists every day
my car must be parked somewhere.
In the boot a raincoat
my gun and some shopping – it's parked awkwardly
but that's what you get
when you're in a hurry.

ATTEMPT AT AN INTERVIEW

'Welcome to the television studios, no, keep on looking at me. Did you ha'
good journey?'

'Easy-peasy.'

'How should I address you?'

'Super hoe. Big Elephant – Cyclone's also OK.
Friends call me Shaka, thank god
I don't have any friends: make up something chic
and it becomes exclusive and now a question for you.
What's it like listening to me?'

'Good question and now a question for you:
What has the king contributed to this life?'

'Rhyme and rhythm. Rhythm and rhyme. Symmetry!'

'And what else?'

'Seems more than enough to me.'

'You embody poetry?'

'I don't ask myself that and what in fact is poetry nowadays.'

'That's a quote.'

'That's a quote!'

'Rhyme and rhythm, that brings me to the following.

We found a few old acquaintances of yours who were prepared to, yes
they're here, there behind that door there
you haven't seen them for a very long time
they're a bit jumpy and slightly mutilated – what's wrong?'

'This isn't what we agreed.
I said no surprises
no tribunal.'

'They've travelled a long way
they're bursting at the seams and then: all those hardships, that outcry
those memories, the producers thought
maybe their stories will shed a different light on things...'

Shaka rips off the microphone, pushes his chair back
and rushes past the cameras and the audience to the exit.

Dripping wet I lie here panting next to a very deep swimming pool.
I think it's around dinnertime now
the sky is grey with coal dust and still I see something move.
I can't quite figure it out, it must be a spot of light
shining bright inside my brain.
My body is full of ants, spiders, woodlice –
funny, a rat is gnawing frantically at my vocabulary
I can hear it working away like it's behind a concrete wall
with a steel door in that wall
that keeps on shutting.
Hush, I think.
All that bellowing the whole night that's me.
At first I thought it was a kind of prayer
but why should I pray, what I own is meaningless.
The water looks like a swamp
a thick soup of algae, leaves and bird poo
I swam and swam as though I'd escaped
and nowhere land in sight.
After which the wind suddenly dropped
and I pulled myself up onto the tiles a winner.
I glanced back for a moment –
miles of empty expanse
then I collapsed.

SHAKA SLOWLY TURNS INTO AN EXTRATERRESTRIAL OBJECT.
The day N lay down something
escaped from him and never returned.
What was left is a chunk of rock
with human characteristics
but without the ability to differentiate.
An apple is a pear is a banana.
A calf is a canary is a horse.
An outstretched hand is a trail of blood
to the outhouse is a disarming
smile is a gruesome murder.
Like a huffy toddler he has mirrors
hung up in all his rooms
to put an end to his sleepless nights.
A warrior who returns from battle
but without a weapon without even a cut
or a graze can wave his life goodbye.
Shaka cries, 'The weakest links must be exterminated.'
Shaka cries, 'Dear subjects We have to pull out the weeds.
Untangle the lot. Do some thorough gardening.'
But fear doesn't unite, angst isn't superglue.
It works more like a shredder.
Look at all those prunings
and limbs everywhere.

7:20   Suspect S darts through the back door of the courts heavily guarded.

7:41   In front of the main entrance the queue of journalists meanders like a spastic snake.

8:13   @SimonH06. Managed it! Sitting in the 4th row! Scrumpled up next to his mother on the 1st. *#motherS*

8:34   Prosecutor enters, shouting in the corridors.

8:39   Defence sets up a laptop for a PowerPoint presentation.

8:55   Here comes the judge, everyone stands.

8:56   Someone shouts, 'Hang the king by his balls.' The woman (was it a woman) is carted off.

8:57   @JWalters. Fooled! Dark figure on the front row is a doppelganger. *#courtcaseS*

9:01   Someone shouts, 'No bail for the king!' They're carted away too.

9:02   There's the real S, the photographers rush towards him.

9:04   Flashing & clicking, the judge asks S how he's doing. See the first photos here.

9:05   'I have to rediscover what I'm good at, your honour,' S whispers.

9:07   The charges are read out solemnly.

9:15   S burst into tears, probably not for the first time.

9:19   Prosecutor quotes something S said to the papers, 'Subjects are simple to replace like disposable people.'

9:25　PowerPoint shows photos of a serious waterfall a sky-blue sea, a couple on the beach a zebra that indolently slaps away a fly with its tail.

9:42　@SimonH06 Judge looks tiredly at his watch. *#courtcaseS*

9:45　On a slide S smiles at a girl on his knee with a strong resemblance to him.

9:51　S lays his head on his mother's lap like a beaten dog.

9:59　Judge asks S if he followed what was said. 'It's all swelling here inside but also out there,' he says softly.

10:01　S's lawyer, 'Let's imagine if S was still alive. He'd be able to give our sick economy a leg up!'

10:02　Giggling from the audience, judge asks for explanation of all that bloodthirstiness.

10:13　Lawyer, 'The way you're looking at the king, that's just not right! No one singing a song for him, it's scandalous!'

10:14　Maximum sentence due to premeditative nature of the crime.

10:16　@JWalters. Everyone shocked! S collapses shattering like a wine glass on the floor. *#remorse*

10:18　Lawyer pulls himself together. 'No one is immortal your honour.'

10:21　S blows his nose – sounds like intestinal gas playing up. Judge visibly represses a smile.

10:23　'So I walk into the hut, rush towards her... this seems to me as clear as day!' the prosecutor cries.

10:31　@Lesser2B. Premeditated or not, that's the question. *#royaldrama*

10:42   Hearing is adjourned, mad rush to the front row but S is whisked away.

10:43   Mother stays sitting there like a widow.

10:58   Judge is back, a laughing S is brought back to his seat.

11:03   S and mother deep in prayer. Drumroll at the back of the room.

11:04   @JWalters. Sitting adjourned again! This time S stays put! *#motherS*

11:08   @JWalters. Toilet break probably – judge already back. *#courtcaseS*

11:12   Time for the defence and S stands.

11:16   S doesn't understand why he's a suspect if he's innocent.

11:18   'I know nothing about human beings and what I think or do cannot be copied by any creature.'

11:21   'You see behind you a picture taken by my mother. I'm showing a lump of gold to the camera and smiling.'

11:22   'That was a good day, I hacked gold from stone, putting my own life at risk. I also sang my Hacking song.'

11:23   'There's gold everywhere, I just have to see it but when I can't find anything, I can't find anything for a long time.'

11:24   'I was chased away as a poor little kid – where will I be buried when I die?'

11:25   Total silence in court.

11:27 'The almighty is oppressing me: exonerate me and nothing will happen to you.'

11:28 Judge clears his throat and mutters something.

11:31 @SimonH06. Silence continues! When is someone going to dare to speak? *#thriller*

11:34 S begins to quote something, Job 31 by the sounds of it. In its entirety.

11:40 Testimonies have dried up, judge suspends the hearing.

12:14 Judge is back, the sentence is: freed on bail, pandemonium breaks out.

12:16 The prosecutor flings his papers on the floor. The forensic expert lights a cigarette. The lawyer calmly closes his laptop.

12:18 @Lesser2B. S amidst the chaos that has broken out. His arms in the air, he doesn't look happy. *#courtcaseS*

12:37 Outside the court S and his mother slip into a blacked out car.

12:39 Excited photographers and cheering supporters run alongside the car for quite a long way before the car speeds to an unknown destination.

The microphones are arranged in a row I've taken my seat.
As though a hand that breaks through the dimensions
grabs my throat and squeezes it shut.
I hear something crack but I don't feel any pain.
I only taste a bit of blood, a metallic glow
and nothing much, you won't hear me complaining.
My body is a temple, a marvel
of technology and spotless.
An appliance on the ceiling transmits warm air inside
the strip lighting hums softly, I hum softly along –
I'm not so easily put off my stride.
I stand up again and brace myself
a small woodpecker in a concrete tree.
Alas, I say Alas I don't have an answer to that.
Out of the corner of my eye I see a butterfly fluttering around the room
I just have time to think How did that get in here
I thought everything was guarded –
then it lands on my shoulder.

A SINGLE BULL. BROKEN FREE
from the herd of bulls
thundering crazily through the streets.
Blind and deaf and bleeding like a heart.
Red eyes, red skin and red mind.
Knocks a mother with a pushchair.
Knocks a cyclist, rams into a bus.
Jumps over ditches, races through red.
Overtakes a tram, batters and topples a chip stall.

Shaka hunts everything that moves.
From outer space an alien would make out
a rapidly spreading blot of inky-black ink.
Accompanied by a crackling voice-over.
'Invalids, toddlers, fiancés, pensioners.
All get to meet the Short Spear.
If you can't tie your laces you'll be killed.
If you don't know how much bread costs at the bakery.
If you weigh too much or too little.
Animal flesh becomes human flesh becomes animal flesh.
The now conquered area once was green and fertile
like a pleasure garden; behind Shaka's back we see
a smouldering steppe, dark as cancer.
The famous depictions of Shaka as an apocalyptic horseman
stem from these times.'
Shaka hears whispering and rustling, stifled voices.
The question is: are we deaf
or can we hear it too?

The mountain pass is notorious.
On the left the tangles of the pine trees
and on the right the planets and stars.
Sometimes I was overtaken, sometimes I had to brake
black-brown clouds charged along ahead of me
as though I should hurry but I was in no hurry.
I drove upwards like in a children's song.
One sharp bend to go and then the highest point of the pass –
a few seconds as light as a skeleton
before everything goes tearing downhill.
I accelerated a bit and held my breath ready
when suddenly I was overcome
by a deep sleep, as clammy as thick fog.
All sound was silenced.
I quickly threw her into second and forced
though I'd existed a moment ago
like a velvet drill in heavenly matter.
Whether I was on my way home, or alone
or accompanied – I've clean forgotten.
Apart from that it was the depth of winter
and then that road, that hateful road
that just keeps on climbing and climbing
there is no end to it.

HIGH TIME THAT SHAKA VISITED HIS GP

'Cholesterol, useless stuff. Fatty.
Nestles obediently into the artery walls.
They shrink, clog up.

Fat doesn't dissolve in water or blood, but it does in protein.
No wait, it does in protein, not in water or blood.
In order to transport cholesterol
it is bundled in little balls of protein.
Obesity. Genetic predisposition. Diabetes
a sluggish thyroid gland – are you following me?
All bad news for dear Friend Health.
But you're not fat, do you smoke?

A high measurement can be an outlier.
But our cholesterol levels are subject to natural variation.
More readings are necessary
to gain a reliable picture.'

The doctor looks up from his flyer bifocally.
Frosty vapour issues from his mouth, like
Terence Stamp in *Superman 2* – no, that comparison
doesn't work but Shaka had a poor night's
sleep leading up to this morning.
A shiny information leaflet with pictures
of fatty red blood cells that shoot
down a slide laughing, colour photos
of healthy men and women
to illustrate that mankind will outlive the cockroach.

Dizzy spells, dizzy spells.

Is the doctor grinning now
or was that line around his mouth
a sign of concern?

'High cholesterol
is a risk factor for heart and vascular diseases.
I know this just as you do.
But don't worry about the high result.
The GP, *c'est moi*, ascertains whether you have other risk factors
to see whether your chance of heart and vascular diseases
is increased and whether medicine is needed.'

Then as if caught out the GP grabs with his left hand
the telephone playing a loud and appropriately energetic tune
next to his mug of steaming chamomile tea.

A song without rhythm or chorus.
Horror pop.
A modest hit, long ago.

'Not now, I'm with a client, I'll call you back. No…
I'm hanging up now.'

The GP discharges himself impeccably of his paternal duty.
Stares despondently past Shaka.
At the raindrops on the windowpane
and the massive yellowwood tree.
Has suddenly forgotten
what that man sitting in front of him had come for.

Strange thing is he doesn't hang up.
Stares at the flyer in his right hand and then back to Shaka.

How to make something of this season.
You can't recover the past – you often hear that.
Shaka tries it every day: he could fall at any moment.
Spend the winter elsewhere, perhaps that's a plan.
Like the birds in the village, nameless creations
but a lot of them are hardy.
All of them on the roof together shivering.
Staying for longer until things improve isn't an option.
Yet still they don't move.

'Every day is slow dying, my dear Shaka.
Sometimes I can fix it, sometimes I fix it
sometimes I can lend a hand too, yes.
But on paper, on paper
everything seems to be perfectly alright. Questions?'

Shaka doesn't have any questions.
Like snow melting in the sun.
He's saved in less than 3 minutes.

They stand up in sync
and, warmly, healthy to the core
Shaka firmly shakes the doctor's cast-iron hand.

This barren expanse I crossed with a week's worth of ammunition.
Here I was hitched to a truck
as I roared the first lines of the national anthem.
Only the first lines, for the melody.
Here I learned to slaughter animals
the innards in a burlap sack and chucked onto the fire.
Here the game was to beat death.
Cycling, jumping ditches and here seven kids peed
over me and I lay there until I could get up again
here one summer's evening I ran after her
through the garden – how she laughed, all that low-lying light.
If I don't watch out I'll take a cautious step back
and another step and step by step
I'll step away from me. Only where I'm far away enough
and no longer can hear myself I'll turn around
and begin to run like mad.
How quiet it is today.
As quiet as a forest in winter.
As quiet as a bird, high in the sky.
As quiet as a sleeping whale.

SHAKA WHO SLEEPS WITH HIS SPEAR.
Standing up.
Birds, butterflies, everything that moves dies under his gaze.
He would lose dramatically in a free election.
Anyone who loves him, he sends on a hopeless mission.
To die on the way
or to return, emaciated.
And then those questions and orders.
Bring that mountain over there to my house.
Bring me an edelweiss.
How much is 33445678 times 17578798906 divided by 21.
Who was originally going to play the male lead
in Gone with the Wind.
What am I thinking about right now.

No one has an answer
or can comply with the instructions, aside from two or three –
who end up dead too.

The press room remains empty.
The headquarters deserted.
No one to sing of Shaka's deeds
the fire is dying fast.
Blow, dear subjects, blow!

I can't remember getting up.
Life drives me on and not death death is child's play.
Each day I get a little closer to civilisation
I can tell because the sky is turning as grey as the earth.
I drag my left leg a little.
An old trick that protects me.
It's uphill all the way
my backlog is hopelessly huge
typical of a mortal's work.
I need a push.
So many steps towards the moon
is so many steps towards the truth
equals hocus pocus.
How did I get this far
I'm a DIYer, a patient
a murderer, glowing in an ancient light.
There's no point enjoying the surroundings –
this is an ordinary day in the past.
I walk a bit I think a bit.
Bad luck for anyone who runs into me.

WARRIORS TOPPLE BY THE DOZEN, LIKE FACTORY-
FARMED CHICKENS.
Not by enemy hands.
Es gibt kein Feinde mehr[1].
And the brain is a sponge.
If it dries out then thought hardens
and the heart hardens too, blood
and language games keep Shaka's brain alive.
I am alone.
Am I alone.
Only I am.
I am lonely.

In her wheelchair Shaka's mother bumps along on the sly
to a potential daughter-in-law one afternoon.
As proud as a granny, captured on the security cameras.
When Shaka hears that he has a baby son
he follows his mother in the darkness to the hut
goes inside, fills the entire space
stands at the cradle and the newborn
dies in the freezing cold of his shadow.
Less than a stanza from here Shaka's mother will come to lie
in a footnote for all eternity, stretched out on the ground.
How delineated her supporting role is now.
The plot is in a hurry, there's another version in the making
but Shaka hears a metal gate slam shut
and breaks into a heartrending roar.
Yo yo yo my mother she's dead a light burns
in every house in this house darkness burns.
The nation mourns though by now you can hardly
speak of a nation, you can't even fill a community centre with it.

1 There are no enemies left.

Bursting into tears upon command:
a top notch specimen of method acting.
And anyone who doesn't mourn is hacked down.
Anyone who mourns and thinks about something else at the same time
is hacked down.

It remains a strange mechanism.
Self-destruction.
Self-hatred.
Self-determination.
Self-service.
The solitary nature of the whole business.
And no one has made a back-up of the landscape
a giant steamroller flattened everything.
The earth, deep purple today and empty
is as smooth as an enormous bowling alley.
There comes the first ball.

When I opened the curtains this morning
I didn't recognise the view.
As though I were looking at a lie.
Lively chatter in front of my window
I stayed motionless like a fly in a storm.
I had to get away from here urgently
before someone noticed me before it started to rain and rain
it didn't stop, dripping wet from the rain
dripping wet from dreaming about rain I set to work.
Anonymously and rapidly.
One by one I carried my few possessions
out of the shed
through the garden
to the old street.
When I'd finished the job
I stood in front of my house wasting away.
Even though I'd been the boss, there –
in any case until anyone
had proved the contrary.

SOMEONE HAS MANAGED TO TAKE A PICTURE OF SHAKA'S HENCHMEN. WE'RE TALKING ABOUT A PHOTO OF THE FAT ONE AND THE LITTLE ONE WITH THE NOSE TALKING TO SHAKA'S BUTLER, NEXT TO A TICKET MACHINE IN A CAR PARK. THE PHOTOGRAPHER, WHO WOULD PREFER TO REMAIN ANONYMOUS, CALLED THIS THE HOLY GRAIL OF PHOTOJOURNALISM.

It wasn't exactly easy for the photographer to take his famous photo.
Over the course of 15 years he spent more than 17,000 hours
hunting his prey before he managed to get the men in his viewfinder.
Aside from a few photos he also recorded a short video.
Shaka's henchmen usually hide away
in the woods or in caves.
Until recently people assumed
they were just a fable, part of
a clever marketing strategy.

ANY REQUESTS?
What does the audience want to hear?
By now the fact that Shaka's spear is exhausted
is assumed general knowledge, the guarantee has expired.
Enough fragments we can skip.
Shaka doing the washing up, watering the plants.
Brushing his teeth, looking for small change
at the kiosk for a pack of Camel Lights.
Zapping aimlessly on the sofa.
Shaka in the queue for a visa — now this is getting interesting.
Stands beside a dockside warehouse
on a bitterly cold evening negotiating with some men.
Someone offers him a light.
A little later we see a boat bobbing on the waves
just off the coast, on board the same men from just now
plus Shaka. Woolly hats, long winter coats.
Dark figures, dark water.

Bloodthirstiness is thirst of the highest order.
A spinning top that doesn't start to totter
and roll away under the china cabinet but
turns faster and faster still until it
spins itself into intangibility.

But that's not possible in real life!
Exactly, that's why.

My muscles are paralysed I should get up and pay.
All kinds of things are being announced
Goodnight, I say sleep tight
I can only think about one thing.
My life must have cost a fortune
with all this prosperity, none of it is checked in – what a relief.
Increasingly I started to look like everyone else
there were masses of likenesses.
Skin was where my mouth is, I always missed something
like a man inside a woman inside a man inside a woman.
But then made of flesh and blood.
I knock back the last dregs of coffee
and remain sitting, thick fog floats into the departures hall.
Or am I mistaken in what I see
I can't smell fire
I can't see fire
no one seems to be panicking.
At this time of day no one even sees me.
I might describe this as a miracle.

SHAKA'S ASYLUM-SEEKER'S NIGHTMARE

I

A man a lady.
The word 'and' between them.
Rain, lots of rain.
The lady says to me Walk to the city.
At three in the morning!
And I say City?
A city she says, a big city.
She says There's help there, no, assistance.
That man didn't say a lot.

II

I say Do you know who I am?
Yes sir, it says so in your i-den-ti-ty pa-per-s.
Go and wait on that chair.
Do you know who I am, I say again.
She says You can sit down *there*, sir.
I'd been there for two weeks when
the decision was announced.

III

The judge said Now you're free.
Free to do what, I asked,
Free to go where, I asked.
Freedom of Limited Location was the answer.
And there or here is where I am now – right?

They say We give you an identity
then you can go back.

IV

What does your government say I hear all the time.
You keep asking me *And what does your government say*.
Can you keep a secret: *I* am the government.
Executive Judiciary power, the whole caboodle.
'Caboodle' isn't that what you say here – nice word.
I sleep here, it's not exactly warm, 'warmth' is relative.
This isn't being recorded I hope.

V

I think I have the flu.
I read 'Antibiotics don't help against flu.'
No, not here.
Where I live, they help there.
Herbs too and spells.
'But this isn't home!'
No, it isn't, you can't die here either.
Here everything always gets healed.

A servant I was a firecracker I found this work next to the border.
It is oppressively hot here but secretly
I'm running the entire world. These flavour enhancers, boosters –
oregano coriander nutmeg and table salt of course
always salt, I sprinkle it on almost everything
the people like that here, while at
my peak I could convert the North pole, yes
could plant a flag on the moon.
And how on earth do I find death, the real one
hard and fast, sometimes if I stretch out
on the wet tiles I know full well how it will go.
Not with a sob, not in a tropical rainforest
not snowed in or with my eyes shut.
There's no job title for what I do but sweating I carve out
a motorway towards a fitting end.
There where my mission has already been deemed glorious.
Keep my eyes fixed ahead, talk little.
That way I'll manage it.

The suitcases in the hall the cupboards empty the windows closed
I have nothing left to wish for.
How long did I disappear for days, weeks, a second.
I love you
ghosts through my head like a mantra.
The moon an heirloom so close by
I can take it in my bare hands.
Three cheers for this reunion
for the Ferris wheel planted right next to the sea.
The neon cheerfulness, the teddy bear
that I won at the shooting range with a single shot.
I kept the animal warm under my coat
a grin stitched to his face –
if I cut him open, cotton wadding would bulge from belly, back
he'd keep on smiling, silent and stiff.
The night caught up with me on the way back
the streetlamps along the boulevard a string of pearls
as forgiving as a guide
a bright line of electric light.

When I think back to the city with all that water it's night-time.
I'm standing on the street I can't say where.
I have to go home so I follow the canal hoping for the best.
Just as I'm thinking I'm almost there
a gazelle, snorting with fear
comes running across the black water.
Three hyenas are chasing it as loud as an alarm
fountains of light bursting under their feet.
The natural disaster shoots left behind the bridge
out of sight, then it's quiet. In the daytime
this water doesn't stink, boats glide through the centre
filled with tourists who wave at cyclists
and at everything that moves, also at that man over there
who wants to fly away, it seems
arms spread, darkened by shadows
a wounded bird in panic – it's no coincidence
that the man is me, however frantically I flap
I just don't leave the ground.
And by now I really do want to go home.
It must be somewhere here, I can hardly believe
what I saw there in the pitch dark.

SHAKA ALMOST KNOWS HIS NIGHTMARES OFF BY HEART.
Fortunately he is strict about keeping a diary –
a dreams and recipes book in one
which is how we know about his sleep-
walking, the terse truths.
That his butler and that comic duo
'disappeared without trace'.
Walks out the door, can no longer find his way back
begins to dribble spontaneously, is avoided like the plague.
Sometimes raises his short spear in a reflex.
Paces despondently up and down in front of Central Station
accosts people randomly for food
or money or a chat.
Is lovingly lifted up and up
as though by a down-filled tow-truck
one melodious evening.
Kindly brought back home.

YOU CAN'T COME HERE WITH THE NAKED EYE

'I still have a number of questions.'

'Go ahead then.'

'Smells nice here by the way.'

'I was just about to eat.'

'Alright I'll keep it short, how does it work.
I mean when you fall asleep.
I try with all my might to stay with it but somewhere it goes wrong.
I miss the bus right in front of my nose
the doors close, the bus leaves.
Me running behind it of course!
Me running behind it of course
but I'll never catch up with it.
Yes, if it has to wait for a long time.
For example at the first traffic lights along the route.
That's five streets further.
I'm quite fast but that's too much for me.'

'What else?'

'All those people who side with the American president.
During a press conference.
The president preaches about arms or disarmament
about the shining path out of poverty, out of this vale of tears.
Or sends his greetings to the country that has just
survived an honest election.
Right behind him a battalion of silenced women, men.
Swaying like seaweed.

Are they standing there as an argument?
Does the president know they exist
or would he get the fright of his life if he looked behind him?
Why did that idea never occur to me
typical, me – now it's too late.
On talk shows
on talk shows you often see those same faces.
Ready to imitate the judiciary
their thumbs up or down or their heads nodding.
The prettiest ones, they're always sitting up front.
Zoomed in on by camera 2.'

'Shaka, if you want to ask something, ask away
but please don't give me a lecture.'

'And why when an accident has happened
on the left side of the road
do you get a traffic jam on the right side?
The reverberation of tin-plate on tin-plate dissolves like ice in water.
So there's nothing to see!
Say people have died
then their souls have already scarpered.
Are oncoming cars
battle-weary and heading home
searching for confirmation?
But the car radio's on isn't it?
Is it an homage
to the leaking petrol and the hydraulic scissors tool?
To the inured gaze of the police officers
and the ambulance workers?
Is the blue party lighting that attractive to us?'

'It must be said, you're getting better at expressing yourself.'

'Autocue.
Allows me to keep smiling.'

'Autocue, autobahn, authorial...
That was it?'

'No, well yes I've forgotten what my parents sounded like.
If I could hear their voices again.
Would my father sound like... *this*?
My mother something like... *this*? Or... *that*?
What I come up with I don't recognize – I'm alone
and they are everybody.
Imagine you are wandering through a gigantic hangar
amidst a chorus of theatrical echoes.
Could be straight out of a Hollywood film.
It's one big loop and I can't sing.'

'You're making progress, Shaka, good questions, you can go.
Don't forget to close the front door properly
on your way out
it's been jamming a bit recently.'

I'm making a terrible mess I think.
I can't bring the spoon to my mouth properly
but the guards are patient
with my dog too, he hardly ever bites.
I should give him a name.
I've got nothing else to say after last night.
No one is interested in bad news so
I don't move a muscle, I don't even blink.
What sadness, nothing but mines and graves
for miles around.
If I am new here there is something wrong with my memory that or
I haven't been paying attention –
what takes place in the mind and what happens outside of it.
My arms are itchy, I smell pretty bad.
Sometimes I'm in favour of something, then against
and every now and then I nod my head
just for form's sake.
A single nod is enough.
I don't have much to say anyway.
He-he-hel-lo m-m-my n-name i-i-i-is.
That's as far as I get.

Rocky mountains, rocky fields.
A blinding white sky, a rusty can at my feet.
Six, seven feet away a clean bleached carcass
collapsed beside a weathered wall.
The heat burned my innards to shreds
until all I could do was grin stupidly –
if I were alive I'd kill for a beer
or something edible but hunger is far behind me!
Gradually I have changed
into a quivering dot on the horizon, world's end
where the Saviour paces day and night.
I kick the can and it shoots away
until it has completely disappeared.
The proverbial eye of the hurricane.
A stupid joke by the powers that be.
But horror at the thought that I could suddenly just disappear
luckily isn't horror anymore
all I know is that I've never been this calm
before, so calm it's driving me mad.

ON THE LAST NIGHT SHAKA DREAMS HIS ENTIRE LIFE STORY.
Every war, every death, every orgasm
every ride in his car, every little conversation
with his mother, every time he bathed
in the gurgling river.
Which can mean two things.
1) Shaka's memory is as strong as steel.
2) He is suffering from severe metal fatigue.
Here and there a person is hacked down
but all of this is impotence.
When the sunlight gingerly peeks out
over the edge of the world
we see Shaka lying in bed for longer than usual.
Hours later when he tries to get up
he immediately collapses on his paws.
His fur is dingy and drab.

A hot air balloon gains height
behind a massive mountainside.
Smaller and smaller, an inverted tear
resolving into the landscape like a riddle.

The nights are the worst.
In the distance the last farms
but I don't recognize a thing, not even my own voice.
Nothing makes sense anymore, nothing –
things suddenly seem dangerously close and recorded.
The water in the ditches, the wind through the knee-high grass
the porous earth and that horse over there
I think it's a horse.
I do up my laces to buy time.
In my rucksack: water, food, dry clothes
a handful of bullets my mobile still has a signal.
I barely reflect, barely breathe.
As though I were dead but I'm bursting with life.
If I'm thirsty, I drink.
If I'm tired, I sing a song
my mother used to sing to me.
From above this might look like running away
but everything is dark from above.
A few miles at the most, I guess
then the sun will come up
gleaming, clear light all around.

FATHER AND MOTHER. N. HALF-BROTHERS
and henchmen. His guards and his women.
His murderers and victims – everyone
shuffles along to shake Shaka's hand.
He humbly accepts their condolences
and there is coffee, tea and homemade cake
the sun shines timidly
the queue is endless, all the way into to the unknown with
now and then a sea of fire or a wedding somewhere.
With people on the beach and people in the cities.
In the countryside and in their cars.
In their beds, in offices, in factories.
Then a highly infectious laugh starts up on the left
the laughter surges, expands
it drowns out longings and loss
flowers unfold, birds fly up
and thousands of millions break
right through the sound barrier.
Then Shaka is free.

His body is found in a field.
Tinged green but perfectly intact.
So poisonous that no animal dares take a bite.

I can't sleep frosty night light is keeping me awake.
I rock back and forth like the leaf of a tree
this rocking brings no repose.
My paws shoot out in a gluttonous reflex
but I'm sated, I've been abandoned in this primeval forest
with its sunburnt trees –
drunk with tiredness after all that I have destroyed.
It was like plodding along an endless dirt track
in noxious heat.
Dotted about between the tree trunks and bushes
bits of humans, fractured or melted.
People say there are ghosts here people say
Things that don't move must be frozen in terror.
But I only feel love
like in an ancient fairy tale.
If I raise myself I pray, I'll pray then and so I pray
and I pray that someone will hear my prayer.
Sirens swell beyond the horizon.
I searched for You but found no resistance.

'EMERGENCY SERVICES, HOW CAN I HELP.'

'Are you receiving me you're speaking to [unclear].'

'Emergency services. How can I help.'

'I wanted to make something from nothing but brilliance and… and… I'm in [unclear] difficult situation [unclear] I'm approximately 2 miles from [unclear] I have to…'

'I can't hear you very well, could you repeat that please.'

'[unclear] be rescued.'

'Could you repeat that please.'

'My [unclear]. I'm finished.'

AFTERWORD

I was partly inspired in the writing of *Man Animal Thing* by
several historical texts. By far my most important source was
the novel *Chaka, An Historical Romance* by the South African
writer Thomas Mofolo (1876-1948). I consulted both the
1931 edition and Chris Swanepoel's translation into Afrikaans
from 1974.

Background reading included *Lessons on Leadership by Terror,
Finding Shaka Zulu in the Attic* by Manfred F.R. Kets de Vries
(2005); *The Washing of the Spears: A History of the Rise of the
Zulu Nation under Shaka and its Fall in the Zulu War of 1879* by
Donald R. Morris (1965); *Talk of the Devil: Encounters with
Seven Dictators* by Riccardo Orizio (2003); *The Soviet UFO
Files* by Paul Stonehill (1998); and *Dinner With Mugabe* by
Heidi Holland (2011 reprint).

The quotes 'The blade of the assegaai was...' and 'People
who were found guilty of sorcery...' on pages 11 and 13 were
taken from *Lessons on Leadership by Terror*.